Of Palm Trees and Skies

Of Palm Trees and Skies

Dr. Afra Atiq

First published in 2024 by Emirates Literature Foundation Publishing LLC
PO Box 24506, Dubai, UAE
1 3 5 7 9 10 8 6 4 2
Publishing Manager: Shurooq Kamal Gewaily

ISBN: 978-9948-738-50-3
Approved by the National Media Council UAE:
MC-02-01-5862891

www.elfpublishing.me

For Mom and Baba, my families near and far,
it is only fitting that this is in your loving honor. To little Afra, who always believed in stories.

To all the dreamers, past, present, and future.
To the poems, all the poems, still to be written
The ones that never made it to paper
The ones that could never find the words, too many or not enough
To the poems that say, welcome home.

CONTENTS

Fajr

Fajr arrives
    on a silver skyline echoing
    off the silence.
    I pray,
    on knees filled with weary thoughts,
    to be anything other than the quiet.
    I pray,
    anchoring my faith to the dawn.

Palms turned upwards towards the sky.
    I pray,
    for everything.
    For poems beneath the doubt,
    that wake up
    the sleepy silence.

في هذا البيت
(In this House, We Learned to Be)

The bookshelf still stands,
all splintered and stubborn pride.
It doesn't
match the rest of the furniture
and can't support any weight.

في هذا البيت
Somehow, we always knew,
mismatched furniture
was a small sacrifice to make
for the wood that reminds us
that our roots go deep.
The bookshelf stands against time,
like an ode,
unchanged.

في هذا البيت
Baba, with that look in his eyes,
says, *"She's my wife of 40+ years"*
My *"equally better half"*

في هذا البيت
we pray,
for each other.

في هذا البيت
everything says
this is where we learned
to be.

Sayer Yaay
(This poem takes its name from a form of Talli)

Threads wrapped around wood,
metallics and colors,
weaving stories through Talli.
Practice and patience
Stories and narratives, intertwined
سلامة علمتنا كيف نروي القصص
Language, lyrical and poetic
Talli - *Sayer Yaay*
Like tides we watch, for four months and ten days
And this, too, is why we must write
Why we must remember

Thread A moves over *thread B*
Or does it loop around like a conversation unsaid?
It is a prayer residing in a heart of faith
I remind myself of my heart of faith
The sky, somehow, seems wider now
As if we were meant to see
all of the horizon in a glance briefly,
But completely
Najm Suhail adorning a map
I don't know which stars they followed
Or which will bring them back
And this, too is why we must write to remember

So let this be your reminder
Let this be your ode after the many, many, metaphors.
In spite of odds and circumstance
And the pages that do not wish you to write
So write
Remember and write
Until each letter reminds you
What it means to rise

Lifeline 2.0

My imagination like wildfire
Vivid as my first memory
I was 2, maybe 3
Sitting on the living room carpet
The dictionary in it's deep blue splendor,
In front of me
Flipping pages and glancing over words
Like somehow I knew these letters and ink would carry me
At 10
Words spiraling into armor
Some words spoken, some not, some silent and buried with weary hands
And some.
Would transform into poems 12 years later
On stages I never dare even dream of
Like somewhere I knew
That if light travels in a straight line
Then the lines of a poem must also travel in infinite and opposite directions
That regardless of the degree of darkness
Syllables will always make words
and words will always make poems
And poems will always lifeline into places we cannot yet reach
Which is to say that, sometimes there is nothing but words
Letters strung together
Illuminating even the most silent of spaces
To lift and teach

وربما
يتبع النور القصيدة كما تتبع القصيدة الكلمات

My favorite lessons have always been about light

As if to say this, too, is Why we Must
(After Dubai Calligraphy Biennale 2023)

The way language flows,
letters lean, as if growing
towards sunlight. Directions grasping at the impossible,
and in between.
Present and previous.
Languages and script, as if to say,
yes, this too,
is why we must
Write.

Learning to Read

When I say my mother
taught me how to read.

I mean that I learned kindness
in same way I learned to read difficult words
by, practicing, and repeating
after her.

شمال
(It Was Always the way)

If you ask Baba
about the direction of home, he will probably say Shamal.
As in, north. As in, a wind we know so well.
As in, rain will be here soon. Surely, blessings will be here soon.

In my house, we know this to be
when Baba cooks Jareesh.
At the first sign of rain clouds,
we know he is already wondering if we have enough crushed wheat
in the storage room, or if he needs to go to the store.

At the first tap of sprinkles on the windows of our home, we know
he is calculating how long it will take to cook. And listing how many
houses
he will send this dish to. He says, maybe, we can make a salad. Because,
"The vegetables in the garden are doing good baba, extra good."

If you ask my father about ingredients and measurements,
he will tell you,
"I am cooking from my heart. I made this from my heart, baba."
This is always the way.
To never make the same dish, the same way, twice.
But to always make the same dish, for the same reason.
This was always his way.

At the first sign of a Shamal wind, we know so well.
I wrote this from my heart, too, Baba.

Water, Flour, Salt, Saffron

One.

We sift through the culinary archives
of our memories
Unearthing stories through ingredients

ماي
ملح
طحين
زعفران

water,
salt,
flour,
saffron,
in specific amounts,
like long overdue conversations.

Two.

I am wondering what made me agree
to do a live cooking demonstration
in front of an audience.
I tell my mother that I need a recipe that is
us

She says,

Balaleet, maybe?
I say no, that's for special occasions
and it feels strange to make it outside of Eid

صالونة سمج

like the one our family makes?

Or

صالونة لحم

Like the one I make?

عيش و صالونة

It is how I know I am home

Three.

My mom wrote down my yedo's Gaimat recipe
on paper now tattered and older than me.
Maps, histories,

water,
salt,
flour,
yeast,
eggs,

Recipes like
long lost letters to ourselves.
A reminder that we are home.

Roots in the Direction of Somewhere

At some point you will be told
That there is no point
No one reads anymore
That if you put a book on a
shelf no one will look at twice

They will tell you that poet
isn't a proper job description

But we

Have seen writers turn words into bridges
Language leaning towards the sun

كلمات تحرك الخيال

In every possible direction

Still
You will hear
that no one reads anymore
There is no point
reason for poems
no shore for a sea of syllables
Set against a backdrop of art

ما في داعي للوزن و القافية

Yet we know better
Than to look at a sky
and not see the makings of a story
We look at the earth
and see the beginning of a ghaf tree
Leaves like chapters
Outstretched like echoes

Somewhere my students ask me
Why do you write
And honestly I don't know
But I can't let them know this
So instead
I tell them

I write because I must
Because 7-year-old me wanted to be a novelist
And 15-year-old me did not believe
she was always a poet
And 30-something-year-old me hangs out with publishers

And somewhere

بعيداً عن المعتاد

In all of this there is a story
Somewhere
 a palm tree
And a poet
Somewhere there is a language
There is always language
We must
learn to write
Because we must write
Beginning middle and end
Narrative and story
Pages and pages
Under sky and breeze
Pages and pages planted
Roots immovable in the many directions
Of somewhere
And don't all good stories begin and end

بداية و نهاية

Somewhere.

Guilded Heart

Under the gilded chambers of your heart,
marveling at everywhere it's been,
I wonder if there's room for me.

I'm in awe of the doors, though they are closed.
They're beautiful, carved and painted gold,
veins like delicate wrought iron flower filled trellises
winding
    over smooth
muscle.

Despite the rumors and lack of welcome mat,
I stand at the doorway with a pie in hand.
Because, I know better than to show up
to your home empty handed.

Still, I am
terrified. I wonder if you will like me
because, like me, you are skeptical
of literally everyone -

the past permanently perched upon your shoulders,
a reminder
that you
are not
worthy
of being loved.

A dull ache,
just present, enough to tell you
that no matter how many poems
you write into existence,
love is not
something that is meant for you.

I know you probably won't open the door,
but if you do -

I'd tell you,
I unraveled
to unlock you from your deadlines and meetings.

The six alarms
you set for yourself every morning,
all three minutes apart
because you like odd numbers
and   even   spaces.
I'd find a way to show you
that you are a library with books
for all the words that never made it to poems
because you love bold gestures.
I'd be unafraid to tell you that you laugh, loudly
but with enough joy to fill the horizon
I'd give you this basket overflowing
with everything you needed but never received:
Closure
Assurance
that you are on the right path
Time
only to see that nothing about you was never truly broken
I'd smash all the moments
you thought you weren't good enough
and mosaic them into a sky full of stars
Then,
We'll walk into the people
we will be better for becoming

And yes,
I know you can't make skies out of moments
but you have a flair
for the
imaginative
and I have a wild streak
I know the things you swore
to never to immortalize in your poems -
a broken grandfather clock
a bruised bookshelf
a conversation in the hallway in 7th grade
the crushing weight of this grief
But
one day we'll tell this story at dinner parties
the one about your gilded heart with the carved doors
about how you opened the door and there it was
your face staring back at you
pie and gift basket in hand
endless staircase under your feet
and how we finally said
welcome home,

we've been expecting you.

نخلة
(Nakhla)

Wild and gracefully beautiful are the trees
that learned to grow
in circumstances bigger than themselves.

Sheryan Al Hayat is based around conversations
with my father, inspired by Dubai Creek & set in
the historic neighborhood of Al Shindagha. The poem
has a unique form - it is bilingual & written in three parts,
each part functioning as an individual poem. Together,
these poems also form a longer poem that can be
read left to right, right to left, middle to right &
middle to left. And this is exactly
what I love about poems - the multitudes
& sometimes infinite ways they can be read &
experienced.

شريان الحياة
(Sheryan Al Hayat)

I asked my father
to draw me a map
of the creek

He said,
الخور
connects the city

baba, if you wanted
to get from Deira to Bur Dubai

تاخدين العبرة
٤ آنات
عقب
نص روبية
الحين درهم

we gaze at the creek
low tide, but still
grand and perfect

حب متوارث
I said
أبويه
This is our history
He says صح,
baba

We walked through
the alleyways of Al Shindagha
سكة ورا سكة
Following memories like directions
He says, I know these houses
I taught their sons in the first grade

He says this like no time has passed
like yesterday he was in the classroom
He points across the water
to Al Ahmadiya School

Hands like a compass
He says,
Baba, my school was here
I taught from 75 to 79

البحر
Holds stories like books
and tells them like poetry
Through currents and tides
seemingly rising
and falling like meter

بحور الشعر في قصيدة تخيلتها من زمان

Waves always finding their way
back to the shoreline
back to us
back home
Lineage and legacy
lifeline of water connecting
two sides of the same
heart
When
they ask me why I love
the water, I tell them,
حب متوارث
from my father, his father
and his father's father
من عتيق وجمعة وفرج
we depended on the sea
like our lives depended on it,

Still, They Ask Me About Poetry

يسألوني عن الكلمات و القصائد

About how and why I am a poet,
and I say,
I don't really know.

But when they ask me about poetry,
I imagine my city with its infinite sky and beating heart.
The dome like نجم سهيل
outside all the ordinary
Weaving traditions like Talli

حب متوارث من جيل إلى جيل

A determination anchored in the essence of who we are,
a history in honor of a future we know to be possible.
Befitting of the vision that builds it into being

We are legacy, hope and optimism,
all in equal parts.

القصيدة
و بحورها
و وزنها

And what of the poems?
The everflowing verses

Et la poesie
N'est pas une coincidence de mots
Poetry is never a coincidence of words,
it is always intentional. Still,
they ask me about poetry.

About legacy and the roots of palm trees,
strong and tethered to constant inspiration.
The soul of this poem.
Still,

يسألوني عن الشعر
و جوابي
دائماً
دائماً
دبي

Stories & palm trees
    over generations.
If you want to know
    the past,
ask a poet.

Beyond the breaks,
(After Dubai Calligraphy Biennale 2023)

But who are you,
outside of the poems you imagine
after line breaks and spaces
held only for stanzas. Beyond well-timed wordplay
and crafted similes. If not for syllables, and perfect placements
ink and parchment, words tethered to context
and meaning inviting poems to speak.

Oud is still burning

On the last day we saw her
at the hospital, I was worried
about smelling good.

I was already late, compelled
by comfort
in the ritual of burning incense,

a brief moment of composure
smoke rising and curling,
as I beckon it towards me

for a split
second,
I am somewhere between 5 and 8,

next to my grandmother,
gazing at her
as she takes perfume-soaked tree bark,

and lays it
atop a glowing piece of charcoal
a familiar sizzle in a foiled lined burner,

as the scented smoke
dangles upside down
from the terracotta *medkhan*.

Nothing is untouched,
the smell of oud hugging
everything in the room.

Memory --
tethered,
bound by ritual.

Oud Malaki -- عود ملكي
earthy, regal, unrelenting.
Reserved for special occasions.

At your wedding,
Bint Ateej, she would say to me.
this one *insha'Allah* for your wedding.

Luban -- لبان
tree sap, frankincense, to ward off
the unwelcome

Ward Taif -- ورد طائف
40,000 honey and rosewater fragranced petals
crushed, distilled, and preserved with sea salt

married to a pearl diver,
she wasn't stranger to
preservation and salt.

Dehn oud -- دهن عود
a gift, one tolah, 10ml, deep amber
liquid mixed with sandalwood.

Thailand,
she would say,
only *sandal* from Thailand.

Mukhamareya -- مخمرية
saffron aged 40 days, mixed with glycerin,
dabbed behind the ears, a rite of passage.

Zaafaran -- زعفران
Floral Saffron red bleeding into orange,
the reason I am late

I revel in the solace of familiarity.
Her golden *burqaa*
with the perfect middle crease on the dresser

Her floral *jallabeya*,
scent of oud
still lingering in the fabric.

Dainty gold threads embroidered
on the cuffs and neckline
like the softest lullaby

Even, when disease
came knocking on her bones
Oud is still burning

Gahwa, still warm
strong, bitter,
undertones of cardamom boiled twice.

Poured with the left hand, offered with the right.
Serve others, *before*
you serve yourself, she would say.

I say *Yedo*,
The perfumer has new oud.
Faransi, this season

she said nothing,
I know she knew
but somehow,

I ended up
here
Late

terrified
to walk the halls
of the hospital I was born in

everyone went somewhere
to call the nurses,
to find consolation

I am in this moment
with her
seeing death

at her bedside
the same place
where I came to life

I whisper to her:
>   *Ya bint Khamis* (Oh, daughter of Khamis)
>   *Ya ajmal ayyami* (Oh, you are the best of my days)
at home,
I open the glass box
of oud,

light
the charcoal until
the glow distracts my eyes,

drop
the perfume-soaked tree bark
in the terracotta *medkhan*

and wait, and wait
for the comfort
of ritual to fall over me.

Wish you were here
(or at least not gone)

My memory wants to send you postcards,
wishing you were here.

I wish you were here.
Or, at least, not gone
Too soon and too far

Remembering
a time, that one time
before there was poetry
and so much silence
That one time
The last time
we didn't know it was the last time
When you were here
Before you suddenly were not
Once, you said I was good at finding things
I still haven't found somewhere to put this grief
Because it is, grief
It is, heavy
and messy and follows me everywhere and never makes any sense
But it's all I have left of you
and I still
wish you were here.

Where do good poets who write bad poetry go?

Where will we keep all this bad poetry?
How do we keep it from tainting all the good-
poetry, how do we keep the secret of the poet?
I often find myself wondering where good poets who write bad poetry
go.
Perhaps, back to their poetry home,
the first place they tried to build words into a house,

The first memory of a poem forming beneath a stained-glass ceiling in
an empty house
Maybe, they try to salvage the ashes of ink and burned manuscripts
they called not worthy of poetry
The English literature major who declared they would not entertain
my poetry on their bookshelves
Until I won an award, now she sits across from me at dinner parties
and tells her fellows how she always knew I was "good"
Which makes me think that bad poetry is destined to live caged
between quotation marks as a "poet"

To never wander into the midst of a non-quotation marks poet
To stay just beyond the fences of the perfectly curated bookshelf
poetry houses
Always needing to find excuses to leave places you never wanted to go
Instead, you find the street corners with the odd poetry
Where they host poetry readings and no experience is required to be
considered good
Have the time of your life and think, if you wished hard enough, this
could be home

Maybe this could be home
There are no questions or literary interrogations in this house of poetry
Go

As far as the stretch of image and imagination will take you, go
Knowing that even if you write bad poems, you can always come home
Back to the poetry
Bad poems can come from good poets
Blood, brick and ink to build this house
Of you, on pillars of bad and good

Imagine the best of the good
Imagine how many discarded words and poets
Never dared to poetry poems of their houses
Into a home
Thinking that a bad poet
Comes from writing bad poetry

Good does not always mean finding a home
Go, for you are a poet
Lay poetry like foundation to the place that says to all poems,
This is your house.

House of Glass

I've always been way too good
with aiming my words.
Time tells me to trust it,
but it lives in a house made of glass.
I am still picking shards of you out of my poems.

You're, Carefully Calculated

That time your teacher wrote,
"youre on the last page of the story",
without an apostrophe.

You contained yourself for three whole minutes, then stood up.
Spine straight as the point you were about to make,
striding to the blackboard to place a carefully calculated apostrophe
halfway between the letters u and r.

You didn't know it then,
but the unyielding way you love language is the first conversation,
of the first relationship,
of the first time you fall in love
with spelling and poems.

Always Like Everyone is Listening
(I Must be heard and to be heard I must be loud)

I was raised never to yell,
told to never shout unless I absolutely had to.
But how do you even say things without yelling?

I must be heard, and to be heard, I must be loud.
For poetry performances,
they give you just three minutes.
Start the clock. Three minutes to make you care about something,
to feel something.

Two minutes and a half,
I told my life story and still, nobody is listening.
So I yell going against everything I was taught.
My bones know I'm not supposed to be yelling.

Never shout,
unless you absolutely have to. Bearing the wounds
of generations, passed down, like hand me down clothes.
Battle scars from being told
to sit down,
be quiet,
be silent,
be still,
be unnoticed,
speak only when spoken to.

I must be loud,
I need my voice to carry.
Be the loudest in the room.
Because, being loud means you are being heard.

Remember your words, Afra.
And for the first time in my life,

I am speechless. Forgetting the words that live
in the crevices of my vocabulary.
I must be heard and to be heard I must be loud.
Because what are words, if they're not known.

ليش ما تعرفين عفراء؟
Be known, Afra,
be loud,
be anything other than other,
loud enough to tell them
this isn't how the story goes.

There is no right answer,
this is what makes up my nightmares.
Recurring conversations saying,
she's just re-writing rhyming words.

Use your words, Afra.
No,
this is the remix.
A reminder that I can take your
just, your only, and give it new context

Poet and scholar,
equal parts of PhD and poetry.
Paper to voice,
vocally, verbalizing
verbs in my vernacular.

Which is
particularly perplexing to parts of people
who try to pack poets into parcels
and padlock them shut.

I'll take your *just* a poet and rise
in language,
in لغة,

in la langue,
من
اللغة إلى المشاعر إلى الشعر إلى القصد إلى القصة

I will take everything
to tell this story,
until my voice bends perception.

I will walk onto stages and tell you
to speak like everyone is listening.
Speak like everyone is listening.
Speak like everyone is listening,
from mountain tops to valleys in places
that you've never heard of,
like they don't know what your words will become.

30 seconds left, Afra
feel your voice grow
from your lungs.
Remember your words, Afra.
Use your words, Afra

Truth spoken through
marble spine made of poems.
Flex your vocal chords
Always
like everyone is listening.

Safi, 10 per Kilo

At the fish market
I remember exactly two things:
The smell
And the verses from vendors

صافي الكيلو على 10
بياح الكيلو على 15
شعري الكيلو على 5 ربيات

Back and forth
Somewhere between thoughts
we stop
And my father says

بابا هذا زين حق المالح

We were both raised to know the ocean
To know Najm Suhail
Also means fishing season
To love the land, to know here and now
Will become stories of then and there
He says love the land
Understand your environment
Know the stars and the ocean
I tell him
Insh'Allah baba
27 years later
I can only wonder if the ocean likes poetry
If it knows we swim metaphors
like currents
to stories, to this house
this bait, this poem

Fireworks

The memories end
up like fireworks.
Endless in light
sparks among stars
this ending, too,
nothing less than beautiful.

Six minutes, Maybe We Write Today

The lines,
here and not here, maybe, possibly
and all at once

Lines on loop
13.19 million times
a remix of things unwritten
gears on shift
never ending
scribbles, barely scratching the surface

We write,
because we need
because we should and do
because we create
because we were told we couldn't
because maybe it's not for you
because it was never meant to be
because it was never the right thing
because we couldn't say it
because we wanted to say it
because we did say it
because thoughts were not enough

But always enough, because

شعر
قصايد
نثر
قصة

Because there are no words
for the smell of oud on a Friday

because there's no word to mean
the heaviness of this light
Because sometimes you can only write
because maybe today is not the day
because they told us (not) to

We write
because maybe tomorrow
because not now
because there's never a right time

Somehow,
we write
because we must
and we erase
because we think
we should.

How Much Does a Heart Have to Hold?

Where do I put all *this*?
How do I disassemble *this* and turn the parts into something worth
saving
Where do I put this heart
asking how much more it needs to hold
This "it gets better",
but not really
this sorrow,
overflowing like riverbeds
on knees filled with a grief
I cannot name
because language is too small
and meaning is not quite big enough

Bless, strong, dense, and heavy

Bless these bones
strong, dense and heavy.
Bless these bookshelf shoulders,
all knowledge and responsibilities.
Bless this one more day.
Bless the hands
of the clock that tell stories
with elaborate hand gestures.
Bless the time there was nothing
to give.
Bless time there was enough.
Bless the never and always enough.
Bless this mind,
always looking for something.
Believing, somehow this could work.
Bless the somehow this could work.

Sometimes, it is to be Grateful

For a beating heart,
these
working
overtime lungs,
and shoulders clasping
a collarbone
holding a voice full of stories.
And with every prayer
Ameen -
Louder than silence
Ameen -
Every single time
Ameen
Upwards turned palms to the sky
Ameen -

Heartfelt Thanks

Thank you for reading this book. Thank you for allowing this poetry to exist, in and outside of the margins.

About the Poet

Dr. Afra Atiq is an Emirati scholar, poet and teaching artist. She earned her PhD in the Creative Industries and holds a master's degree in diplomacy. She lives and writes in the city of Dubai. *Of Palm Trees and Skies* is her debut poetry collection.

www.ingramcontent.com/pod-product-compliance
Lightning Source LLC
Chambersburg PA
CBHW020939160726
47993CB00007B/2852